Baby Names and Meanings

Find out The Most Suitable Name Meanings for Your Baby

Copyright © 2020

All rights reserved.

DEDICATION

The author and publisher have provided this e-book to you for your personal use only. You may not make this e-book publicly available in any way. Copyright infringement is against the law. If you believe the copy of this e-book you are reading infringes on the author's copyright, please notify the publisher at: https://us.macmillan.com/piracy

Contents

How to Choose a Name for Your Baby 1

10 Tips To Picking The Perfect Baby Name 8

100 Trending Baby Names of 2020 16

1000 Most Popular Last Names in the U.S and Meaning 22

Top 300 Baby Girl Names in the U.S 83

Top 300 Baby Boy Names in the U.S 88

5 Naming Trends From Around The World 94

How to Choose a Name for Your Baby

Baby Names Tips for Picking a First, Middle, and Last Name

Choosing your baby's name is an important decision you have to make as a parent. It can be fun, but the responsibility of naming another human being can make it a bit intimidating. After all, your child will carry that name throughout their life.

You may already have a good idea of what you're looking for in a name. But, your partner, family, and friends may have a few opinions of their own. It can definitely be tough to get everyone on the same page. It doesn't have to be a stressful experience, though. It can be very enjoyable. Here you'll find information and tips for getting through it and picking the perfect name for your baby—even if you're thinking about more unique names for your baby.

You may have a long list of girl names, boy names, and gender-neutral names already started by the time you find out you're expecting, but not everyone does. Some parents start from scratch with each child, and some even wait until the baby is born to choose a name. Each parent finds inspiration differently.

Choosing Baby Names

Many expectant parents begin with a specific category in mind, and there are many categories to consider.

Family Names

- Grandparent's names
- Mother's maiden name
- Juniors or III, IV
- Family traditions

Cultural or Ethnic Names

- Japanese
- Italian
- Greek
- Irish

- French
- Spanish
- Hawaiian
- Jewish
- Russian
- Native American
- African

Place Names

- Countries
- Cities
- States

Names From Pop Culture

- Actors
- Movie characters
- Book characters
- Television characters
- Video game characters
- Musicians
- Songs
- Artists
- Disney
- Athletes
- Politicians

Religious Names

- Christian
- Jewish
- Muslim
- Virtue Names
- Spiritual Names

Other Popular Categories

- Seasons
- Nature
- Colors
- Mythology
- Astrology
- History

And many, many, more.

It might seem overwhelming, but there are ways to narrow it down. You can go through an alphabetical list of names in a book and check off the ones you like, or you can choose a name you find appealing and look for others that are similar. You can also get your list started by asking family and friends for suggestions, or you can pick a category of names and go from there. There's not a right or wrong way to do it, so go with what works for you and your partner. If one way doesn't seem to be going too well, then switch it up and try something else.

Choosing a Middle Name

You don't have to give your child a middle name. However, the vast majority of American families prefer to give one to their baby.1 The nice thing about it is that most people feel less stressed over the middle name.

The middle name has a few practical uses. For parents who give their child a family name that others in the family also have, a middle name helps to provide the child with a separate identity (cousins John Robert, John Joseph, and John Christopher can all feel as though they have their own name even though they are all named after grandpa). A middle name is also the perfect place to hide the family name that you're choosing out of obligation and not because you love it. Or, it can be a place to have a little bit of fun. If you're going with a more formal first name, the middle name can be more creative or unique. Or, if you're choosing a very unusual first name, the middle name can be more traditional.

A middle name is also a great place to put a safety name or a fallback name for your child to use later in life in case they don't love their first name. If you choose a gender-neutral first name for your child, you can add a gender-specific middle name such as Avery Duane or Sydney Elizabeth. It gives kids options as they grow. If it's necessary, being able to fall back on a traditional middle name can help boost your child's self-esteem and self-confidence too.

Choosing a Last Name

When it comes to your child's last name, you may not have a choice. In some states and countries, the baby must be given the father's last name, if known.2

Sometimes it has to be the mother's last name. Other places allow for more options, especially if mom and dad aren't married.

Some families have parents with different last names who hyphenate them to indicate the joining of the two families (e.g., Mary Smith-Jones). Other families choose to combine parts of each parent's last name to make a new last name (e.g., Davis and Anderson = Daverson or Andervis). And, some families do not use either parent's last name. Instead, they give their child a completely different last name.

10 Tips To Picking The Perfect Baby Name

Deciding on your baby's name is one of the most enjoyable things you can think about during pregnancy.

Whether you already have a few names in mind or you're waiting until after the birth, here's our top 10 tips to choosing a name for your new baby.

1. WANT TO KEEP WITHIN A FAMILY TRADITION?

If you want to keep with tradition and use an old family name for your baby, but you don't want it to be their first name you could always try using it as a middle name instead. Sometimes a family surname can make for an unusual first name – like Taylor or Cooper for example.

2. IT'S A LIFE-LONG THING

Remember that your child has to carry this name for their whole life so it should suit all ages – A sweet name for a little girl may not suit when she's an adult. Likewise what may sound ideal for a gurgly baby boy may not be as cute on a grown man.

3. FUTURE-PROOF IT!

It's also worth considering baby names trends. Names that are popular today may mean your child will share a class with lots of others of the same name. While copying celebrity baby names may seem like a cool thing to do now, they may look dated in a few years time.

4. STUCK FOR INSPIRATION?

Try a name based upon its meaning. If your baby girl was born in late December, you could call her Natalie, which means born at Christmas, or if your son has a shock of auburn hair, Russell, meaning little red haired man could be appropriate. It's always worth checking out the meaning of a name you like, in case it's meaning is not quite what you had in mind!

5. TRADITIONAL SPELLINGS MAY BE BEST!

While you may fall in love with an unusual or unique spelling of a traditional name – Jaxon for Jackson or Sofiah for Sophia, remember that it can cause confusion – and make life more difficult for your child when they are young. Stick with traditional spelling – your child can always change the spelling later.

6. HAVE MORE THAN ONE CHILD?

If you have more than one child, you may want to link their names to your new arrival in some way. You could choose names with a shared heritage, such as Biblical or Gaelic names, using the same or similar middle names, or picking one that begins with the same letter – although rhyming them could be a bit too cutesy!

7. SAY THE FULL NAME OUT LOUD!

Is it easy to say? Does it sound right? Does it spell out something unintentionally amusing - like C. Shells? Does it balance out your surname? A long surname, for instance, can happily take a short forename and vice versa (eg John Christopher, Christopher John).

8. THINK ABOUT NICKNAMES

Always think about possible nicknames and shortened versions that could arise from your baby's name: the name Elizabeth is bound to be shortened to Betty, Liz or Lizzie – do you like all the versions? Or does the name shorten to an unfortunate nickname that your child will find hard to live with?

9. WHAT DO THE INITIALS SPELL OUT?

If you're planning to give a child one or more middle names, always consider what the initials spell out. David Oliver Patrick Evans may sound like an impressive name for your baby boy, but he'll be very lucky if he avoids being called DOPE at school! Charlotte Olivia Weston sounds lovely – but trust us, the initials COW won't pass unnoticed when she's school aged.

10. SHHH! KEEP IT A SECRET!

By all means ask family and friends for their opinion – but it's often best not telling them your favourite name until after the baby is born. This way you'll avoid hearing any negative stories (like Aunt Flo who hates it because it reminds her of a horrible girl at school etc) that could put you off. No one will quibble with your choice of name once the baby arrives.

Unique Baby Names

Parents are opting toward more unique baby names now more than ever. According to our baby survey of over 400,000 parents, many responded that they want to avoid the top 10 baby names. Many parents don't want their child to be "one of five Aidans in his class."

Choosing a unique baby name requires considering your child's future individuality while also keeping in mind situations where an uncommon name may affect them, such as in school or work situations... think about the ease of spelling and pronunciation for these types of settings.

Here is a list of the more unique baby names. These names were highly rated, but are not in the top 100 in U.S. births.

Unique Girl Names

Looking for a unique girl name for your baby? Your child's name is one of the many important decisions you make when having a child-- why not make it special? Unique names have become more popular in recent years, after generations of Ashleys, Sarahs, and Jennifers. While there is nothing wrong with choosing a common name, picking a unique girl name will set her apart and help her gain a bit of individuality among her peers.

Baby Names and Meanings

Aadi	Aaralyn	Abana
Abarne	Abeni	Abia
Abiba	Abilene	Abra
Abrianna	Abrienda	Acacia
Acadia	Accalia	Aceline
Acelynn	Adabella	Adah
Adalia	Adalira	Adamina
Adamma	Adara	Adaya
Addo	Addy	Adel
Adelie	Adelle	Adelphie
Adena	Adeola	Aderes
Aderyn	Adia	Adie
Adila	Adina	Adita
Adoncia	Adonia	Adonica
Adora	Adrina	Adsila
Ady	Aelwen	Aerilyn
Aerith	Aeron	Aerona
Aeryn	Afia	Afrodille
Agalia	Agape	Agatha
Aggie	Aglaia	Ahava
Ai	Aideen	Aiko

Unique Boy Names

While you may face pressure from friends and family, choosing a unique boy name for your baby is an extremely personal and important choice for your child. It can set them apart, helping them obtain individuality among their peers. Even still, you may be struggling with the balance of "not so common" but also "not too unique" that it imparts an inconvenience to your child.

Abba	Abbott	Abdukrahman
Abhay	Abie	Abner
Absolom	Acton	Adarsh
Addae	Ade	Adelio
Adem	Adish	Adit
Adlai	Adli	Admon
Adolf	Adonai	Adri
Adriano	Adwin	Adymn
Agamemnon	Agostino	Ahanu
Aidric	Aimon	Airell
Ajani	Ajax	Ajay
Akamu	Akio	Akiva
Akuji	Alagan	Alair
Alastair	Alban	Albin
Albus	Aldan	Aldon
Alem	Aleron	Alexavier
Alexei	Algernon	Aloysius
Alrik	Altan	Alvar
Amadeus	Aman	Amando
Amar	Amergin	Amil

Unique Baby Names - Gender Neutral

Using a gender neutral name is already a distinctive choice-- though becoming more common now-- but maybe you want to take it one step further and choose a unique gender neutral name. These names don't fit into a box when it comes to naming conventions of any kind.

Abcde	Achava	Acotas
Adair	Adiel	Adler
Aero	Africa	Aiken
Aindrea	Ainslie	Aj
Akia	Alabama	Alary
Alaula	Albany	Aldis
Alexi	Alick	Aloha
Alohilani	Americus	Ames
Amethyst	Ameya	Amiel
Amor	Amory	An
Ananda	Andie	Andren
Aniston	Anstice	Aolani
Aquarius	Aquinnah	Ardin
Aren	Arien	Arion
Arius	Arizona	Arrian
Arrow	Artemis	Artemus
Ash	Ashby	Ashland
Asmara	Astin	Atlee
Auburn	Auden	Audi
Aulani	Aulii	Aure
Auren	Aurum	Avalon

100 Trending Baby Names of 2020

Since there was a delay in the Social Security Administration top baby names list for 2019, we've decided to tabulate the top 100 trending baby names of 2020 (so far). This list is calculated from our user's favorite name lists, from December 1, 2019 through May 9, 2020. Any surprises?

Rank	Boy Names	Girl Names
1	Oliver	Charlotte
2	Liam	Ava
3	Ethan	Amelia/Emilia
4	Aiden/Aidan	Olivia
5	Gabriel	Aurora
6	Caleb	Violet

7	Theodore	Luna
8	Declan	Hazel
9	Owen	Chloe
10	Elijah	Aria/Arya
11	Henry	Scarlett
12	Jackson/Jaxon	Isla
13	Grayson/Greyson	Abigail
14	Levi	Freya/Freja
15	Benjamin	Adeline
16	Finn/Fynn	Sophia/Sofia
17	Miles/Myles	Nora/Norah
18	Alexander	Adelaide
19	Sebastian	Emma
20	Leo	Mila
21	Landon	Lily/Lilly
22	Emmett	Grace
23	Everett	Maeve
24	Milo	Ivy
25	Jasper	Ella
26	Archer	Eleanor
27	Lucas	Audrey

28	Noah	Genevieve
29	Harrison	Iris
30	Hudson	Isabella
31	Felix	Lucy
32	Elliott	Ophelia
33	Jacob	Eloise
34	Atticus	Vivienne/Vivian
35	Lincoln	Lorelei
36	Gavin	Wren
37	Dominic/k	Hannah
38	Jack	Clara
39	Atlas	Lydia
40	Isaac	Madeline/Madeleine
41	Logan	Claire
42	Wyatt	Astrid
43	Silas	Thea
44	Cole	Kaia
45	Theo	Cora
46	Holden	Penelope
47	Luke	Naomi
48	William	Zoey

49	Isaiah	Aaliyah
50	Adrian	Elizabeth
51	Elias	Evangeline
52	Samuel	Autumn
53	Arthur	Esme
54	Gideon	Mia
55	Kaden	Daisy
56	Arlo	Ruby
57	James	Margot
58	Adam	Layla
59	Colton	Anastasia
60	Ronan	Sadie
61	Roman	Stella
62	Asher	Lila
63	Nolan	Rosalie
64	Jonah	Daphne
65	Rhys	Fiona
66	Nathan	Phoebe
67	Axel	Savannah
68	August	Alice
69	Connor	Eliana

70	Xavier	Eliza
71	Charles	Gemma
72	Eli	Arabella
73	Daniel	Athena
74	Nathaniel	Maya
75	Ezra	Saoirse
76	Beau	Zoe
77	Zachary	Sienna
78	Tobias	Evelyn
79	Carter	Rose
80	Matthew	Harper
81	Ian	Josephine
82	Ezekiel	Felicity
83	Aaron	Delilah
84	Thomas	Amaya
85	Xander	Caroline
86	Soren	Olive
87	Oscar	Adalyn
88	Callum	Brielle
89	Nicholas	Matilda
90	Ace	Aurelia

91	Josiah	Willow
92	Michael	Natalie
93	Vincent	Leilani
94	Edward	Ada
95	Lachlan	Elena
96	Chase	Mabel
97	Apollo	Emily
98	David	Isabelle
99	Jace	Nadia
100	Malachi	Amara

1000 Most Popular Last Names in the U.S and Meaning

Here are the top 1000 last names (surnames) in the United States, according to the last U.S. census. Is your family name on the list?

1 SMITH – A smith is a craftsman, and was used for as an occupational title for many different crafts.

2 JOHNSON – Son of John.

3 WILLIAMS – Son or family of William.

4 BROWN – Surname from a nickname for someone with a dark complexion or hair.

5 JONES – From the family of Jon/John.

6 GARCIA – Of unknown meaning.

7 MILLER – Occupational surname for someone who worked in a mill. Grain, wood, etc.

8 DAVIS – Son of David.

9 RODRIGUEZ – Son of Rodrigo.

10 MARTINEZ – Son of Martin.

11 HERNANDEZ – Son of Hernando.

12 LOPEZ – Son of Lope/Lobe, meaning "wolf."

13 GONZALEZ – Son of Gonzalo.

14 WILSON – Son of William.

15 ANDERSON – Son of Andrew.

16 THOMAS – Son of Thomas.

17 TAYLOR – From the family of the tailor.

18 MOORE – A family who lived near a marsh or bog.

19 JACKSON – Son of Jack/John.

20 MARTIN – From the god of Mars.

21 LEE – Family who lived in or near an open meadow or clearing.

22 PEREZ – Son of Pedro (Pedrez/Perez).

23 THOMPSON – Son of Thomas.

24 WHITE – A family of light complexion or hair.

25 HARRIS – Son of Harry.

26 SANCHEZ – Son of Sancho.

27 CLARK – Occupational surname for a clerk.

28 RAMIREZ – Son of Ramiro.

29 LEWIS – Son or family of Lewis.

30 ROBINSON – Son of Robin, a nickname for Robert.

31 WALKER – Occupational surname for a person who walked on damp cloth in order to thicken it.

32 YOUNG – Meaning "the younger." Surname given to a son of a man, when they had the same name.

33 ALLEN – Little rock.

34 KING – Ruler of the area.

35 WRIGHT – Occupational surname meaning a craftsman.

36 SCOTT – From Scotland.

37 TORRES – Family who lived near a tower.

38 NGUYEN – Someone who played a stringed instrument, similar to a lute.

39 HILL – Family who lived near or on a hill.

40 FLORES – Son of Floro.

41 GREEN – Occupational surname for a groundskeeper or family that lived near an open green.

42 ADAMS – Family of Adam.

43 NELSON – Son of Neil.

44 BAKER – Occupational surname for family of a baker.

45 HALL – Occupational or place surname for a person who lived or worked in a hall.

46 RIVERA – From the shore or bank of a river.

47 CAMPBELL – From the Latin De Bello Campo meaning "from the beautiful field." Could also be from a Scottish/Gaelic nickname (cam béul) meaning "crooked or sassy mouth."

48 MITCHELL – Variation on the name Michael, meaning "Who is like God?"

49 CARTER – Occupational surname for a cart driver.

50 ROBERTS – Family of Robert.

51 GOMEZ – Man

52 PHILLIPS – Family of Phillip.

53 EVANS – Family of Evan.

54 TURNER – Occupational surname for someone who worked with a lathe.

55 DIAZ – Son of Diego

56 PARKER – Occupational surname for someone worked as a park keeper or game keeper.

57 CRUZ – Of the Cross – relating to Jesus Christ

58 EDWARDS – Family of Edward

59 COLLINS – Family of Coilean

60 REYES – Literally translated to "Kings," it refers to the phrase "La Virgen de los Reyes," meaning the Virgin of the Kings.

61 STEWART – Occupational surname for someone who was a steward.

62 MORRIS – Dark-skinned, from the Moors.

63 MORALES – By the mulberry tree

64 MURPHY – Irish surname meaning "Descendant of Murchadh."

65 COOK – Occupational surname for a cook/chef.

66 ROGERS – Family of Roger

67 GUTIERREZ – Son of Gutierre.

68 ORTIZ – Son of Orti

69 MORGAN – Welsh surname meaning "by the sea."

70 COOPER – Occupational surname for a barrel maker.

71 PETERSON – Son of Peter.

72 BAILEY – Occupational surname for a bailiff.

73 REED – Red – person with reddish complexion.

74 KELLY – Irish surname meaning "bright headed" or red-headed. From Ó Ceallaigh.

75 HOWARD – Occupational surname for a "ewe herder."

76 RAMOS – Family from the wooded area. From the latin "ramus" meaning "branch."

77 KIM – Korean surname meaning "gold."

78 COX – Occupational surname, a derivative of "Cook"

79 WARD – Guardian

80 RICHARDSON – Son of Richard.

81 WATSON – Son of Walter. (Watt was a nickname for Walter)

82 BROOKS – Family who lived by or near a brook (creek).

83 CHAVEZ – Occupational surname for a key maker.

84 WOOD – Lives in or near the woods.

85 JAMES – Family of James (Supplanter).

86 BENNETT – Family of Benedict (Blessed).

87 GRAY – From a nickname for someone with gray hair or house.

88 MENDOZA – People who live near or are from the village of Mendoza, Spain. Basque term meaning "Cold Mountain."

89 RUIZ – Son of Ruy or Roy.

90 HUGHES – Family of Hugh.

91 PRICE – Family of Rhys.

92 ALVAREZ – Family of Alvaro.

93 CASTILLO – Lives in or near the Castle.

94 SANDERS – Family of Alexander.

95 PATEL – Indian/Gujarati surname meaning "Landowner."

96 MYERS – Occupational surname for a Mayor.

97 LONG – Surname from a nickname for someone who was tall.

98 ROSS – Scottish surname indicating someone who lived on or near a point of high land that juts out into a large body of water.

99 FOSTER – Occupational surname, a contraction of "Forester."

100 JIMENEZ – Son of Jim/James.

101 POWELL – Son of Hywell.

102 JENKINS – Son of John.

103 PERRY – Son of Harry.

104 RUSSELL – Little Red one.

105 SULLIVAN – Irish surname from descendant of Ó Súileabhán (Little Dark Eyes)

106 BELL – Occupational surname for a bell-ringer/news announcer. "Hear ye! Hear ye!"

107 COLEMAN – Son of Colum.

108 BUTLER – Occupational surname for a butler/wine steward.

109 HENDERSON – Son of Hendrick/Hendry.

110 BARNES – Someone who lived or worked in or near a barn.

111 GONZALES – Son/Family of Gonzalo.

112 FISHER – Occupational surname for fisherman.

113 VASQUEZ – Son of Vasco.

114 SIMMONS – Family of Simon.

115 ROMERO – From or traveler to Rome.

116 JORDAN – From the area of the River Jordan.

117 PATTERSON – Son of Patrick.

118 ALEXANDER – Defending Men – possibly an occupational surname for a soldier.

119 HAMILTON – From the crooked hill.

120 GRAHAM – People who lived in or near a "gravelly homestead" – a contraction of the name Grantham (like Downton Abbey)

121 REYNOLDS – Family or son of Reginald, or the King (rey).

122 GRIFFIN – Mythological creature with the body, tail, and back legs of a lion.

123 WALLACE – Welsh or Foreigner.

124 MORENO – Brown-skinned.

125 WEST – From the West.

126 COLE – From the word "coal" indicating a coal miner or possibly someone with darker skin.

127 HAYES – Lives in or near an enclosure.

128 BRYANT – Family of Brian.

129 HERRERA – Occupational surname for an iron worker (ferrier).

130 GIBSON – Son of Gilbert (nicknamed Gib).

131 ELLIS – Son or Famiy of Elijah/Elias

132 TRAN – Vietnamese surname meaning old, ancient.

133 MEDINA – From the city.

134 AGUILAR – From a place name, meaning "Eagle."

135 STEVENS – Son of Steven.

136 MURRAY – Scottish place name from the area of Moray, meaning "seaboard settlement."

137 FORD – Lives by a shallow place in the river.

138 CASTRO – Portuguese/Spanish surname meaning "Castle."

139 MARSHALL – Occupational surname for someone who is a lawman or takes care of horses.

140 OWENS – Son of Owen.

141 HARRISON – Son of harry.

142 FERNANDEZ – Son of Fernando

143 McDONALD – Son/family of Donald

144 WOODS – Family who lived in or near the woods.

145 WASHINGTON – From the area belonging to Wassa's people. Wassa was a feminine Anglo-Saxon given name.

146 KENNEDY – Irish surname, from Ó Cinnéidigh, meaning Misshapen or ugly head – might be derived from someone who wore a helmet so much their head was misshapen.

147 WELLS – From the well spring or water hole.

148 VARGAS – From the pasture.

149 HENRY – Ruler of the Home.

150 CHEN – Chinese surname meaning "morning."

151 FREEMAN – A person who was not owned or ruled by another.

152 WEBB – Occupational surname from the name webber, meaning "weaver."

153 TUCKER – Occupational surname for someone for a "cloth thickener."

154 GUZMAN – Lived in or near the town of Guzmán, Spain.

155 BURNS – Lives by the stream. From Old English word, burna.

156 CRAWFORD – By the river/ford crossing

157 OLSON – Son of Olaf.

158 SIMPSON – Son of Simon.

159 PORTER – Occupational surname for someone who transported items.

160 HUNTER – Occupational surname for an animal hunter/trapper.

161 GORDON – Scottish surname meaning "spacious fort or home."

162 MENDEZ – Contraction of Menendez, meaning son of Mendo.

163 SILVA – Portuguese surname meaning by the woods or forest.

164 SHAW – Family who lived near a dense wooded area.

165 SNYDER – Occupational surname for a clothing tailor.

166 MASON – Occupational surname for a bricklayer.

167 DIXON – Son of Dick/Richard.

168 MUÑOZ – Son of Muño, a personal name that means "hill."

169 HUNT – Hunter.

170 HICKS – Family of Richard.

171 HOLMES – Lives near a small island or islet.

172 PALMER – Pilgrim.

173 WAGNER – Occupational surname for a wagon maker.

174 BLACK – Person who is darker in complexion.

175 ROBERTSON – Son of Robert.

176 BOYD – Scottish surname, from the Celtic term "boidhe" meaning fair or yellow.

177 ROSE – Lives near the roses.

178 STONE – Occupational surname for someone who worked with stone, or a family who lived near a stony area.

179 SALAZAR – From Salazar, Spain. Salazar literally translates to "old hall."

180 FOX – Cunning like a fox, or a person with red hair.

181 WARREN – Lives near a warren/animal enclosure.

182 MILLS – Occupational surname for one who lived near or worked in a mill.

183 MEYER – Mayor.

184 RICE – Welsh surname meaning "fiery warrior" based on the name Rhys.

185 SCHMIDT – Occupational surname, German form of Smith – meaning ironworker or tradesman.

186 GARZA – The heron bird.

187 DANIELS – Family of Daniel.

188 FERGUSON – Son of Fergus.

189 NICHOLS – Family of Nicholas.

190 STEPHENS – Family of Stephen.

191 SOTO – Lives in or near the small forest.

192 WEAVER – Occupational surname for a weaver of cloth.

193 RYAN – Irish surname and given name meaning "descendant of a follower of Rían"

194 GARDNER – Occupational surname for a gardener/groundskeeper.

195 PAYNE – Originally meaning pagan.

196 GRANT – Large, great.

197 DUNN – Dark or brown in complexion.

198 KELLEY – Irish surname meaning "bright headed" or red-headed. From Ó Ceallaigh.

199 SPENCER – Occupational surname for a butler or steward of a manor.

200 HAWKINS – From the hawk's place.

201 ARNOLD – Power of the Eagle.

202 PIERCE – Family of Peter.

203 VAZQUEZ – Son of Vasco.

204 HANSEN – Son of Hans.

205 PETERS – Family o Peter.

206 SANTOS – Saints or Family of Santo.

207 HART – Irish surname, from the Gaelic Ó hAirt meaning 'descendant of Art.'

208 BRADLEY – From the broad meadow.

209 KNIGHT – Occupational surname for a knight or someone who worked in a knight's household.

210 ELLIOTT – Family of Elias.

211 CUNNINGHAM – Scottish surname from the Gaelic Ó Cuinneagáin meaning "descendant of the leader."

212 DUNCAN – Irish surname from the Gaelic meaning "brown chief."

213 ARMSTRONG – Literally means strong man.

214 HUDSON – Son of Hugh.

215 CARROLL – Irish surname from the Gaelic "O Cearbhaill" meaning "fierce in battle."

216 LANE – Irish surname from O'Laighin, meaning the descendant of Laighean.

217 RILEY – From the rye clearing.

218 ANDREWS – Family of Andrew.

219 ALVARADO – From the white land.

220 RAY – Ray of sunshine, or King.

221 DELGADO – Slender, skinny.

222 BERRY – From the fortress, castle.

223 PERKINS – Son of Peter.

224 HOFFMAN – German occupational surname meaning property manager.

225 JOHNSTON – From John's town.

226 MATTHEWS – Son of Matthew.

227 PEÑA – Lives near the rock or cliff.

228 RICHARDS – Family of Richard.

229 CONTRERAS – From the town of Contreras, Spain. Liiterally means "opposite."

230 WILLIS – Family of William.

231 CARPENTER – Occupational surname for a carpenter.

232 LAWRENCE – Family of Lawrence or from an area named Laurence.

233 SANDOVAL – From Sandoval, Spain. Literally means "land of forest."

234 GUERRERO – Soldier, warrior.

235 GEORGE – Family of George (Farmer).

236 CHAPMAN – Occupational surname meaning tradesperson or merchant.

237 RIOS – Person who lived near the river.

238 ESTRADA – Literally means "street" or "way"

239 ORTEGA – From Ortega, Spain.

240 WATKINS – Family of Walter/Watt

241 GREENE – Lives in or near a green area.

242 NUÑEZ – Son of Nuño

243 WHEELER – Occupational surname for a person who made wagon wheels.

244 VALDEZ – Son of Valdo/Waldo.

245 HARPER – Occupational surname for someone who played or made harps.

246 BURKE – From the burg (town) of the castle.

247 LARSON – Son of Lars.

248 SANTIAGO – Of the Saint Tiago/Diego.

249 MALDONADO – Ill-favored.

250 MORRISON – Son of Morris.

251 FRANKLIN – Free man.

252 CARLSON – Son of Carl.

253 AUSTIN – Family of Augustin/Augustine.

254 DOMINGUEZ – Son of Domingo

255 CARR – From an area of wet, rough ground

256 LAWSON – Son of Lawrence

257 JACOBS – Family of Jacobs

258 O'BRIEN – Of the Family of Brien

259 LYNCH – Anglicized version of the Irish surname Ó Loingsigh, meaning "descendant of the mariner."

260 SINGH – Lion-like.

261 VEGA – From the plain, meadow.

262 BISHOP – Occupational surname for a bishop.

263 MONTGOMERY – From a mountain name in France.

264 OLIVER – Elf Army

265 JENSEN – Son of Jens

266 HARVEY – Worthy of Battle.

267 WILLIAMSON – Son of William

268 GILBERT – Bright Pledge.

269 DEAN – From the valley.

270 SIMS – Family of Simon.

271 ESPINOZA – From the thorny area.

272 HOWELL – Anglicized form of the Welsh Hywel, meaning "eminent."

273 LI – Chinese surname meaning Plum or Plum Tree.

274 WONG – Variation of the Korean surname Huang, which literally means "shiny" or "yellow."

275 REID – Red-headed or had a ruddy complexion.

276 HANSON – Son of Hans.

277 LE – Vietnamese surname meaning lives near a pear tree.

278 McCOY – Anglicized form of a Scottish surname meaning son of Aodh.

279 GARRETT – Family of Gerald.

280 BURTON – From the fortified town.

281 FULLER – Occupational surname for someone who washed cloth in the clothmaking process.

282 WANG – Chinese surname meaning "king."

283 WEBER – German occupational surname for a weaver.

284 WELCH – From the same root as "Welsh," meaning foreigner.

285 ROJAS – Red-headed or ruddy complexion.

286 LUCAS – From Lucania, Italy.

287 MARQUEZ – Son of Marco.

288 FIELDS – Lived in or near the fields.

289 PARK – Korean surname, meaning "gourd."

290 YANG – Chinese surname meaning "willow tree or aspen."

291 LITTLE – Surname from a nick name meaning little man.

292 BANKS – Lives near hillside or ridge.

293 PADILLA – Place name, literally means "saucepan or little pot."

294 DAY – From the family of David.

295 WALSH – Welsh, foreigner, stranger – referring to Celt.

296 BOWMAN – Occupational surname for an archer.

297 SCHULTZ – Occupational surname for a judge or mayor.

298 LUNA – From one of the towns named Luna in Spain. Literally means "moon."

299 FOWLER – Occupational surname for someone who works with fowl (birds).

300 MEJIA – Unknown meaning, might be a religious surname referring to the Messiah.

301 DAVIDSON – Son of David.

302 ACOSTA – From the coastal region.

303 BREWER – Occupational surname for a brewer (beer or ale maker).

304 MAY – Family of Matthew.

305 HOLLAND – From the Netherlands/Holland.

306 JUAREZ – Son of Suero. Variation of Suarez.

307 NEWMAN – Stranger, newcomer.

308 PEARSON – Son of Piers.

309 CURTIS – Person with manners. Courteous.

310 CORTÉZ – Person with manners. Courteous.

311 DOUGLAS – From the dark or green river.

312 SCHNEIDER – Occupational surname for a tailor.

313 JOSEPH – He will add.

314 BARRETT – Warlike person, quarrelsome.

315 NAVARRO – Person from Navarre, France.

316 FIGUEROA – Lives near the fig tree.

317 KELLER – German occupational surname for a winemaker.

318 ÁVILA – From the city of Avila, Spain.

319 WADE – By the ford.

320 MOLINA – Occupational surname for a miller.

321 STANLEY – Lives near the stone clearing.

322 HOPKINS – From the family of Hob (nickname for Robert).

323 CAMPOS – Lives in or near the countryside.

324 BARNETT – From the place near the clearing (burned place).

325 BATES – Son of Bartholomew.

326 CHAMBERS – Occupational surname, servant who worked the bedrooms or chambers.

327 CALDWELL – Lives by the cold well.

328 BECK – Leaves by the stream.

329 LAMBERT – From the bright land.

330 MIRANDA – Place name, meaning a family who had a great (physical) view or outlook.

331 BYRD – Occupational surname for someone who worked with birds.

332 CRAIG – Lives near the outcropping of rocks.

333 AYALA – Lives near the hillside or pasture.

334 LOWE – Lives on or near the prominent, small hill.

335 FRAZIER – Scottish clan surname, meaning varies but possibly "near the strawberry field."

336 POWERS – A person or family who came from the town of Poix in France.

337 NEAL – Son of Niall, literally meaning "cloud" or "champion."

338 LEONARD – With the strength of a lion.

339 GREGORY – Possibly from "Gregorian" monks, literally means "watchful, awake."

340 CARRILLO – Spanish surname, literally means "cheek." From cart/wagon, so it may be occupational.

341 SUTTON – From the South.

342 FLEMING – Flemish (Belgian/Dutch) person or from Flanders, Belgium.

343 RHODES – From a clearing in the woods

344 SHELTON – From the ledge/enclosure. Place name.

345 SCHWARTZ – Person of dark or swarthy complexion. Literally means "black."

346 NORRIS – From the North. Northerner.

347 JENNINGS – Family of "little" John.

348 WATTS – Family of Walter.

349 DURAN – Literally means durable, hard. Perhaps to describe a person who is steadfast or stubborn.

350 WALTERS – Family of Walter.

351 COHEN – Occupational Hebrew surname for a priest.

352 McDANIEL – Son of Daniel.

353 MORAN – Sea Warriors.

354 PARKS – Living in or near a green area, or occupational surname for a groundskeeper.

355 STEELE – Occupational name for a foundry/steel worker.

356 VAUGHN – From the Welsh "fychan" meaning small, little

357 BECKER – Either an occupational surname meaning "baker" or used for a family who lived by a stream.

358 HOLT – Lives by or near the woodlands.

359 DELEON – Family of Leon.

360 BARKER – Occupational surname for someone who either tanned leather (from the bark of a tree), or from the Old French Berchier, which was a shepherd.

361 TERRY – Power of the Theudo people.

362 HALE – From the remote valley.

363 LEON – Lion-like.

364 HAIL – From the remote valley.

365 BENSON – Son of Benjamin.

366 HAYNES – Enclosure.

367 HORTON – From the farm on muddy soil.

368 MILES – Son of Mile.

369 LYONS – Son or family of Lyon.

370 PHAM – Vietnamese surame meaning "extensive."

371 GRAVES – Occupational surname for a steward, from from Middle English word "greyve."

372 BUSH – Lives near the bush or thicket.

373 THORNTON – Lives in or near the town with thorns.

374 WOLFE – Wolf or Wolf-like.

375 WARNER – Guard.

376 CABRERA – From the place of goats.

377 McKINNEY – Form of the Gaelic "Mac Cionaodha" meaning son of Cionaodha (pagan god of fire).

378 MANN – Strong, manly.

379 ZIMMERMAN – Occupational surname for a master carpenter.

380 DAWSON – Son of David. Daw was a nickname for David.

381 LARA – Spanish habitational surname for someone who came from Lara de los Infantes, a small community in the province of Burgos, Spain.

382 FLETCHER – Folk army.

383 PAGE – English occupational surname for a page.

384 McCARTHY – Form of the Gaelic "Mac Carthaigh" meaning son of Carthach (loving).

385 LOVE – From the French "louve" meaning a female wolf.

386 ROBLES – From the village of Robles, in the province of Leon, Spain. Literally means "oak."

387 CERVANTES – From old Spanish meaning "servant" or the word ciervo, meaning "stag" or a "woman's man."

388 SOLIS – From the village or town of Soler.

389 ERICKSON – Son of Eric.

390 REEVES – Occupational surname meaning sheriff or local official.

391 CHANG – Chinese surname with many meanings. One being an occupational surname for a bow maker.

392 KLEIN – Small.

393 SALINAS – Lives in a large building or fortress.

394 FUENTES – Fountains.

395 BALDWIN – Brave friend.

396 DANIEL – God is my judge.

397 SIMON – One who harkens.

398 VELASQUEZ – Son of Velasco.

399 HARDY – Bold, Courageous.

400 HIGGINS – From the Irish surname Ó Huiginn meaning "descendant of Uigin" (Viking).

401 AGUIRRE – From a prominent place.

402 LIN – Chines surname meaning "from the forest."

403 CUMMINGS – Possibly from the French town Comines.

404 CHANDLER – Occupational surname for a candle-maker.

405 SHARP – Smart person.

406 BARBER – Occupational surname for a barber.

407 BOWEN – Welsh surname meaning Son of Owain.

408 OCHOA – Basque surname meaning "The wolf."

409 DENNIS – Family of Dennis.

410 ROBBINS – Family of Robin.

411 LIU – Chinese surnmae meaning "to kill, destroy."

412 RAMSEY – Locational surname from the town of Ramsey, UK.

413 FRANCIS – Person from France or "free man."

414 GRIFFITH – Leader with a strong Grip.

415 PAUL – Small.

416 BLAIR – Battlefield.

417 O'CONNOR – Son of Connor.

418 CARDENAS – From the land of thorns.

419 PACHECO – Noble one, or person from France.

420 CROSS – Locational for someone who lived near a crossing, or occupational for someone who carried a cross in church.

421 CALDERON – Spanish occupational surname for one who makes or sells cooking vessels (i.e. cauldrons).

422 QUINN – An Anglicized form of the Gaelic surname O' Cuinn, meaning "counsel."

423 MOSS – A contraction of the name Moses, meaning "born of a god."

424 SWANSON – Son of Swan or an occupational surname for a herdsman (swain).

425 CHAN – Chinese surname literally meaning field or plain.

426 RIVAS – From the sea side or river bank.

427 KHAN – Chief, ruler.

428 RODGERS – Family of Roger.

429 SERRANO – Lives near a mountain ridge or collection of hills.

430 FITZGERALD – Son of Gerald.

431 ROSALES – From the place of roses.

432 STEVENSON – Son of Steven.

433 CHRISTENSEN – Son of Christian.

434 MANNING – Strong, valiant.

435 GILL – Nickname for William.

436 CURRY – Locational surname for families from a town named Curry.

437 McLAUGHLIN – Son of Lochlann, meaning "lake land."

438 HARMON – Form of the name Herman, meaning "army man."

439 McGEE – Gaelic surname meaning "Son of Aodh," meaning "fire."

440 GROSS – Big, large.

441 DOYLE – Irish surname from the Gaelic "Dhubh-ghall" meaning "dark stranger."

442 GARNER – Contraction of Gardener or occupational surname for someone who was in charge of the storehouse (granary).

443 NEWTON – From the new town.

444 BURGESS – Free man of a fortified town.

445 REESE – From the given name Rhys, meaning "enthusiasm, passion."

446 WALTON – From the walled town.

447 BLAKE – White complected or white haired.

448 TRUJILLO – Family from the city of Trujillo, Spain. Literally means citadel of Julian (Turro-Julio).

449 ADKINS – Family or son of Adam.

450 BRADY – Possibly from the Gaelic surname "Mac Bradaigh" son of the thief, or from the early English "brad-eage" meaning "broad eye" or someone with excellent eyesight.

451 GOODMAN – Man of god, or landowner.

452 ROMAN – Person from Rome, Italy.

453 WEBSTER – Occupational surname for a weaver.

454 GOODWIN – Good friend.

455 FISCHER – Fisherman.

456 HUANG – Chinese surname that means "bright" or "yellow."

457 POTTER – Occupational surname for someone who made pottery.

458 DELACRUZ – Literally translates to "of the cross."

459 MONTOYA – From the hills and valleys.

460 TODD – Fox.

461 WU – Chinese surname meaning "gateway to heaven."

462 HINES – Occupational surname for a deer keeper or tender.

463 MULLINS – French occupational surname for someone who worked in a mill.

464 CASTANEDA – Literally translates to "chestnut," and might have been used to describe a person with reddish-brown hair or worked a chestnut grove.

465 MALONE – From the Gaelic surname "O'Maoileoin" meaning follower of St. John.

466 CANNON – Occupational surname for someone who worked at a house of clergy.

467 TATE – Cheerful person.

468 MACK – Son of…

469 SHERMAN – Literally translates to "shear man," an occupational surname for someone who trimmed pills off the surface of fine cloth.

470 HUBBARD – Variation of the name Hubert, meaning "bright heart."

471 HODGES – Family of Roger.

472 ZHANG – Chinese surname meaning "archer."

473 GUERRA – Literally means "war," used for a stubborn person or soldier.

474 WOLF – Son of Wolfgang.

475 VALENCIA – From Valencia, Spain. Means "valor, courage."

476 SAUNDERS – Family of Alexander.

476 FRANCO – Person from France.

478 ROWE – Locational surname of someone who lived by a "row" of something, or from Rowland, meaning "Renowned Wolf."

479 GALLAGHER – Irish surname meaning descendant of Gallchobhair. Literally means "foreign help."

480 FARMER – Occupational surname for a person who worked a farm.

481 HAMMOND – From the Norse Viking name "Hamundr," meaning "high protection."

482 HAMPTON – From the town near the water meadow.

483 TOWNSEND – From the end of the town (town's end).

484 INGRAM – People from England.

485 WISE – Wise or educated person.

486 GALLEGOS – Foreigners.

487 CLARKE – Occupational surname for a clerk.

488 BARTON – From the barley town.

489 SCHROEDER – German occupational surname for a tailor.

490 MAXWELL – From Mack's stream, pool, or well.

491 WATERS – From the place near the water, or family of Walter.

492 LOGAN – From the Irish surname O'Leoghain, meaning "descendant of the warrior."

493 CAMACHO – Twisted or disfigured.

494 STRICKLAND – From the cow pasture.

495 NORMAN – From the northern region of France.

496 PERSON – Son of Per/Peter.

497 COLÓN – Contraction of the name Colombo, meaning "dove."

498 PARSONS – Occupational surname for a parson or priest.

499 FRANK – Person from France.

500 HARRINGTON – From the town of stony ground.

501 GLOVER – Occupational surname for a glove maker or glove merchant.

502 OSBORNE – Viking name, literally meaning "Bear God"

503 BUCHANAN – Locational surname from the area of Buchanan in Stirlingshire, UK. From the Gaelic "buth," meaning house, and "Chanain" meaning of the canon.

504 CASEY – Irish surname from the Gaelic "O'Cathasaigh," meaning "son of Cathasach"

505 FLOYD – From the Welsh Lloyd or Llwyd, meaning "grey."

506 PATTON – Son of Pat.

507 IBARRA – From the valley or hillside.

508 BALL – Descriptive surname for a bald man.

509 TYLER – Occupational surname for a tailor.

510 SUAREZ – From the southern army.

511 BOWERS – Occupational surname for a worker.

512 OROZCO – Habitational name from Orozco, Spain. Literally means "Son of bringer of wisdom."

513 SALAS – Literally means "room, hall." Could be habitational or occupational for someone who worked in a mansion.

514 COBB – Nickname meaning "lump" or a short form of the name Jacob.

515 GIBBS – Family of Gilbert (Gib was a nickname for Gilbert).

516 ANDRADE – Habitational name for people who lived in the small parish of San Martiño de Andrade in the town of Pontedeume, Galicia in Spain.

517 BAUER – Occupational surname for a worker.

518 CONNER – An occupational surname for an inspector of weights and measures. Or a form of the Irish/Celtic name Conchobhair, meaning "Descendant of the Hound/Desire" – possibly meaning "wolf lover."

519 MOODY – One of brave spirit.

520 ESCOBAR – Habitational surname for someone who lived in or near a place overgrown with broom (a shrub with long, thin green stems).

521 McGUIRE – From the Irish surname "Mag Uidhir" meaning "son of Odhar" which literally means "pale-complected."

522 LLOYD – From the Welsh Llwyd, meaning "grey."

523 MUELLER – German occupational surname for a miller or one who works in a mill.

524 HARTMAN – Dutch surname used for a "hardy/strong man."

525 FRENCH – Person from France.

526 KRAMER – Occupational surname for a merchant or shopkeeper.

527 McBRIDE – Son of the servant of Brighid.

528 POPE – Occupational surname. Although it currently means the religious leader of the Catholic church, it was a title used for clergy of any rank.

529 LINDSEY – From Lincolnshire or Lincoln Island.

530 VELAZQUEZ – Son of Velasco.

531 NORTON – From the north town, north settlement.

532 McCORMICK – Son of Cormac.

533 SPARKS – Originally a Norse nickname given to someone with dynamic character, full of life.

534 FLYNN – From the Gaelic surname "O Floinn," literally meaning ruddy or red-haired.

535 YATES – Occupational or habitational surname for someone who was a gate-keeper, or lived near a prominent gate.

536 HOGAN – From the Irish "O Hogain" meaning "descendent of Ógán."

537 MARSH – Family who lived near the marshland.

538 MACIAS – Spanish/Jewish surname meaning "Messiah."

539 VILLANUEVA – From the new town.

540 ZAMORA – Family from the ancient city of Zamora in North West Spain. Literally means "wild olives."

541 PRATT – From the Old English word "praett" meaning a trick (like pratfall). Probably used as a nickname for a magician or jokester.

542 STOKES – From the Old English "stoc" meaning trunk of a tree. Probably a habitational surname for a family who lived near tree stumps.

543 OWEN – Lives by the yew tree, or person who appears youthful.

544 BALLARD – Nickname for a person who had a bald head.

545 LANG – Nickname for a person who was tall.

546 BROCK – Badger or mischievous person.

547 VILLARREAL – From the royal estate/village.

548 CHARLES – Free man.

549 DRAKE – Dragon. Most probably used for someone who was brave and formidable in battle.

550 BARRERA – Family that lived near muddy area or ground of clay.

551 CAIN – Hebrew name meaning "acquired."

552 PATRICK – Nobleman.

553 PIÑEDA – Habitational surname from several places in Spain. Literally means "forest of pines."

554 BURNETT – Descriptive surname for someone with brown hair (brunette).

555 MERCADO – Occupational surname for someone who works in a market.

556 SANTANA – Follower of St. Anna.

557 SHEPHERD – Occupational surname for a herder of sheep.

558 BAUTISTA – Baptist or baptized.

559 ALI – Exalted, revered.

560 SHAFFER – German occupational surname for someone who was a household manager or steward.

561 LAMB – Occupational surname for a herder of sheep.

562 TREVINO – Lives in a house on a boundary, or where boundaries meet.

563 McKENZIE – Scottish Gaelic clan name meaning "Son of Coinneach," literally meaning "fair one."

564 HESS – Person with hood/helmet. Used for families from the region of Hesse, in Germany.

565 BEIL – From the German "bil" meaning axe. Most likely an occupational surname for someone who made axes or used them (like a lumberjack).

566 OLSEN – Son of Olaf.

567 COCHRAN – Scottish surname for a family who lived near the lowlands of Cochrane.

568 MORTON – Scottish surname meaning "from the big hill."

569 NASH – From the place near the ash tree.

570 WILKINS – Family of William.

571 PETERSEN – Son of Peter.

572 BRIGGS – Variation of the name Bridges – could be habitational for someone who lived near a bridge or occupational for someone who built bridges.

573 SHAH – Persian surname meaning "king."

574 ROTH – German surname meaning "red," used for a person with red hair.

575 NICHOLSON – Son of Nicholas.

576 HOLLOWAY – Lives near the holy spring.

577 LOZANO – Italian-Swiss surname for people from the city of Locarno, Switzerland.

578 RANGEL – Spanish/Portuguese surname, meaning unknown.

578 FLOWERS – Occupational surname for someone who works flowers – like a gardener – or with a bow & arrow. The latter derived from the Middle English "flo/fla" meaning arrow, with the addition of the suffix "er" (one who does or works with).

580 HOOVER – From the German Huber, meaning "plot of land or farm."

581 SHORT – Nickname for a short person.

581 ARIAS – Occupational surname either from the Latin "aro" meaning farmer, or a craftsman from the Latin "ars" meaning skill.

583 MORA – Blackberry.

584 VALENZUELA – Habitational surname from several places named Valenzuela in Spain. Literally means "Little Valencia" and Valencia means "bravery, strength."

585 BRYAN – High, Noble.

586 MEYERS – Occupational surname for a mayor.

587 WEISS – German surname element meaning fair hair or pale complected.

588 UNDERWOOD – Literally means "below the trees of a forest," and could be a habitational surname.

589 BASS – Big/tall or an occupational surname for someone who caught or sold fish.

590 GREER – From the family of Gregory.

591 SUMMERS – Occupational surname for a "sumpter" a person who drove pack mules or horses.

592 HOUSTON – From Hugh's town.

593 CARSON – Probably a form of Karsten, or a created name meaning Son of Carr/Kerr.

594 MORROW – From the row of cottages on the moor.

595 CLAYTON – From the village of clay (on clay ground).

596 WHITAKER – From the white field or from the wheat field.

597 DECKER – Occupational surname for a thatcher or roofer.

598 YODER – Swiss surname meaning son or family of Theodore.

599 COLLIER – Occupational surname for someone who sells or burns charcoal.

600 ZUNIGA – From the town of Estuniga, Spain. Meaning near the water channel, strait.

601 CAREY – Welsh surname meaning "from the fort on the hill."

602 WILCOX – Son of William.

603 MELENDEZ – Visigoth surname meaning "Entire Gift."

604 POOLE – Lives near a small lake or stream.

605 ROBERSON – Son of Robert.

606 LARSEN – Son of Lars.

607 CONLEY – From the Gaelic surname "O'Conghaile," meaning "son of the brave hound."

608 DAVENPORT – Habitational surname of families from Davenport in Cheshire, UK. Literally means lives by the stream that leads to the port or bay.

609 COPELAND – Bought land.

610 MASSEY – Matthew's land.

611 LAM – Chinese surname meaning "Forest."

612 HUFF – Lives by a ridge or hollow.

613 ROCHA – Portuguese surname based on the French surname Roche, which means "lives by the rocky crag."

614 CAMERON – Nickname surname meaning "bent nose."

615 JEFFERSON – Son of Jeffery.

616 HOOD – Scottish occupational surname for a maker of hoods or nickname for someone who wore one.

617 MONROE – Scottish clan name possibly meaning "Man from the river Roe" referring to an Irish place name.

618 ANTHONY – Unknown meaning.

619 PITTMAN – Lives by a quarry or pit.

620 HUYNH – Korean surname meaning "bright" or "yellow."

621 RANDALL – Son of Rand/Rande. Literally means "little shield."

622 SINGLETON – Habitational surname of people who lived in a town named Singleton or in or near a burnt clearing.

623 KIRK – Literally means "church" and could be a habitational surname for someone who lived near a church or occupational for someone who worked in a church, like a pastor.

624 COMBS – LIves near a small valley ("cumb").

625 MATHIS – Family of Matthew.

626 CHRISTIAN – Follower of Christ.

627 SKINNER – Occupational surname for someone who made hides or pelts.

628 BRADFORD – From the broad or big ford.

629 RICHARD – Brave ruler.

630 GALVAN – Nickname for someone who had a receding hairline or was going bald.

631 WALL – Lives near a city wall or enclosure.

632 BOONE – Good person or from Bohon, France.

633 KIRBY – Lives near the Church/Farm.

634 WILKINSON – Son of William.

635 BRIDGES – Lives near a bridge or a bridge builder.

636 BRUCE – From various place names in Normandy, France.

637 ATKINSON – Family or son of Adam.

638 VELEZ – Visigoth surname meaning "vigilant people."

639 MEZA – Lives in or near a mesa, plateau.

640 ROY – Royal, Kingly.

641 VINCENT – Conqueror.

642 YORK – From the ancient city or county of York, UK. Literally means "yew tree."

643 HODGE – Pet form of the name Roger.

644 VILLA – Homestead.

645 ABBOTT – Occupational surname for someone employed by or who served as an abbott.

646 ALLISON – Unknown meaning, but possibly "son of Alan."

647 TAPIA – Lives in or behind a mud wall.

648 GATES – Lives in or behind a gated area.

649 CHASE – Nickname given to a skilled huntsman.

650 SOSA – Portuguese surname meaning "from the salt water" (salsa agua)

651 SWEENEY – From the Scottish/Gaelic surname "Mac Suibhne" literally meaning "young warrior from another land."

652 FARRELL – From the Irish surname,"O' Fearghail" literally means "Descendant of the brave man."

653 WYATT – Brave warrior.

654 DALTON – From the town near the valley, dale.

655 HORN – An occupational surname for someone who either played a horn instrument or made small articles, like spoons, out of animal horn.

656 BARRON – Occupational surname for someone with the title of Baron, or a nickname for someone who acts "higher than his station."

657 PHELPS – Family of Phillip.

658 YU – Various meanings.

659 DICKERSON – Son of Richard.

660 HEATH – Lives in or near a heath (open, unculivated land) or from a town named Heath.

661 FOLEY – From the old Gaelic surname, "O'Foghladha," meaning "Descendant of the pirate."

662 ATKINS – Family of Adam.

663 MATHEWS – Family of Matthew.

664 BONILLA – Lives in or near Bonilla in the province of Cuenca, Spain. Literally means "Good little one."

665 ACEVEDO – Spanish surname meaning someone who lives near or in a grove of holly trees or hollywood.

666 BENITEZ – Son of Benito.

667 ZAVALA – From Zawada or Zawady, literally meaning "fortress."

668 HENSLEY – Habitational surname for someone who lived in or near Hensley, UK. Literally means "a woody clearing."

669 GLENN – Lives in or near a valley.

670 CISNEROS – From Cisneros in the province of Palencia, Spain. Literally means "place of swans."

671 HARRELL – Nickname for someone with a good head of thick hair.

672 SHIELDS – From a shed or shelter.

673 RUBIO – Red-headed or someone with a ruddy complexion.

674 HUFFMAN – Man/Steward of a farm.

674 CHOI – Korean surname meaning "one who oversees the land and the mountain."

676 BOYER – Bow maker.

677 GARRISON – Son of Gerard or Gerald.

678 ARROYO – Habitational surname from any of numerous places named Arroyo, literally meaning "water channel or irrigation channel."

679 BOND – Landowner who is bound by loyalty to the local lord.

680 KANE – From the town of Caen, in Normandy, France. Literally means "battlefield."

681 HANCOCK – Son of John.

682 CALLAHAN – From the Gaelic surname "O Ceallachain."

683 DILLON – From or near Dilwyn in Herefordshire, UK. Or a respelling of the Irish "O'Duilleain", meaning "descendant of the blind one."

684 CLINE – From the German "klein" meaning little, small.

685 WIGGINS – Son of the high noble or warrior.

686 GRIMES – Viking surname meaning "masked person, fierce."

687 ARELLANO – Habitational surname for a family from Arellano, spain. Originally from the Latin Aurelianus, which referred to the farm or estate of Aurelius.

688 MELTON – From the middle settlement.

689 O'NEILL – Son of Neill.

690 SAVAGE – Nickname surname for someone who was wild.

691 HO – Chinese surname with several meanings, descriptive of a chin waddle or characteristic "long-lasting."

692 BELTRAN – Spanish surname meaning "bright raven."

693 PITTS – Lives near a hollow or pit.

694 PARRISH – Someone who lives near Paris, France or near a particular "parish" – a geographical area defined by religion.

695 PONCE – Derived from the name Pontius, from the Greek "pontos" meaning ocean.

696 RICH – Wealthy or family of Richard.

697 BOOTH – Lives near a stall or hut.

698 KOCH – German occupational surname for a cook or kitchen manager.

699 GOLDEN – Nickname surname for a blonde person, someone with "golden hair."

700 WARE – Occupational surname for someone who was employed at a weir or dam, or habitational surname for someone who lived near one.

701 BRENNAN – From the Irish surname "O Braonáin," meaning "descendant of Braonán." Literally means "raindrop or drop of moisture."

702 McDOWELL – From the old Gaelic surname, "MacDubhghaill" meaning son of the dark one.

703 MARKS – Family of Mark or Marcus.

704 CANTU – Occupational surname for a singer or cantor.

705 HUMPHREY – From the name elements "hun" meaning "bear cub" and "fried" meaning "peace." Interpreted as "peaceful warrior."

706 BAXTER – Occupational surname meaning a female baker.

707 SAWYER – Occupational surname for a woodsman or someone who worked with a saw.

708 CLAY – Occupational or habitational surname for someone who worked with clay or lived on clay land.

709 TANNER – Occupational surname for someone who tanned hides.

710 HUTCHINSON – Son of hugh, or son of the close, beloved relative.

711 KAUR – Sikh surname meaning "Princess."

712 BERG – From the mountain.

713 WILEY – Habitational surname for families who came from a number of towns in the U.K. named Wiley. Literally translates to the willow woods.

714 GILMORE – From the Celtic surname "MacGille Mhoire," meaning servant of the Virgin Mary.

715 RUSSO – Descriptive surname for someone who was a red-head or had a ruddy complexion.

716 VILLEGAS – From the house near the village.

717 HOBBS – From the family of Hobb, a nickname for Robert.

718 KEITH – Nickname for an offspring or young person.

719 WILKERSON – Kin or son of William.

720 AHMED – Muslim surname meaning "extremely praiseworthy."

721 BEARD – Descriptive surname for a man with a very distinct beard.

722 McCLAIN – Scottish clan name, originally "Mac Gille Eathain," meaning "son of the servant of Saint John."

723 MONTES – Habitational surname for someone who lived on or near a hill/mountain.

724 MATA – Habitational name derived from a number of towns in Spain and Portugal. Literally means "Forest land."

725 ROSARIO – Contraction of the Spanish "María del Rosario," given to a girl who was born on the festival of Our Lady of the Rosary, celebrated on the first Sunday in October.

726 VANG – Scandinavian surname, probably habitational – from a number of farmsteads and other places. Literally means "meadow" or "field."

727 WALTER – Family of Walter.

728 HENSON – Son of Henry.

729 O'NEAL – Son of Neal.

730 MOSLEY – Habitational surname for a family that came from any number of towns named Mosley in the U.K. Unknown meaning.

731 McCLURE – From the Gaelic surname "M'Ill'uidhir," which literally translates as "Son of Ordar's follower."

732 BEASLEY – From the bent grass clearing.

733 STEPHENSON – Son of Stephen.

734 SNOW – Descriptive surname for someone with very pale skin or light blonde hair.

735 HUERTA – Lives by the top of a hill or near a fortress.

736 PRESTON – From the village with the priest. Literally "Priest's Town."

737 VANCE – From a low marshland.

738 BARRY – From the Gaelic surname "O' Baire," meaning the male descendant of Fionnbharr, or fair-haired one.

739 JOHNS – Family of John.

740 EATON – From any number of towns called Eaton in the U.K. Literally means "River enclosure."

741 BLACKWELL – Lives near the black stream.

742 DYER – Occupational surname for someone who dyed either cloth or hair or hide.

743 PRINCE – Nickname surname for someone who acted royal or "above their station."

744 MACDONALD – Son of Donald.

745 SOLOMON – Peaceful one, from the Hebrew "Shalom."

746 GUEVARA – From Guevara, Spain. Literally means "prominent."

747 STAFFORD – From the landing by the ford.

748 ENGLISH – Person from England.

749 HURST – Someone who lives by a wooded hill.

750 WOODARD – Contraction of "Woodward" meaning ward or caretaker of the woods.

751 CORTES – Courteous, refined.

752 SHANNON – From the Gaelic "O'Sionain," an occupational surname for someone who worked with straw.

753 KEMP – Champion. Given to a person who was a champion of a competition such as jousting.

754 NOLAN – From the Gaelic surname "O'Nullain," meaning "son or descendent of the King's herald."

755 McCULLOUGH – From the Scottish clan name, "MacCullaich" meaning "son of the boar," where the boar represented a brave man.

756 MERRITT – Habitational surname for a family who came from Merriott in Somerset, UK. Literally means "the gate at the boundary."

757 MURILLO – Lives near a boundary or wall.

758 MOON – Either from the French word "moun" meaning a monk or someone who lives a monastic lifestyle, or from the Cornish word "mon," meaning "thin" applied to a person who was skinny. Most probably had nothing to do with the actual moon.

759 SALGADO – Galician and Portuguese nickname surname for someone who was witty or wry, from the word salgado meaning "salty."

760 STRONG – Descriptive surname for a person who was physically strong.

761 KLINE – German nickname surname given to someone who was small.

762 CORDOVA – Habitational surname for a family from the ancient city of Córdoba, Spain. Literal meaning unknown.

763 BARAJAS – Habitational surname for a family from any number of villages of that name. Literally means "the watering place."

764 ROACH – From the French surname "Roches," meaning "lives near a rocky crag."

765 ROSAS – Habitational surname for someone who lived near roses, or occupational surname for someone who was a florist or grew roses.

766 WINTERS – Nickname surname for someone who was literally cold or unemotional.

767 JACOBSON – Son of Jacob.

768 LESTER – From Leicester, U.K. or the county town of Leicestershire. Might go back to meaning "campers on the river Legra."

769 KNOX – Near a round-topped hill (cnoc)

770 BULLOCK – From the English word "bullock" meaning young steer. Given to a young person who was excitable or energetic.

771 KERR – From the word "kjarr", meaning wet ground covered with brush.

772 LEACH – Either an occupational surname for someone who worked with leaches (like a doctor) o from the word "loecc/loch" meaning water or lake for someone who lived near one.

773 MEADOWS – Lives in or near the meadow.

774 ORR – Lives near a slope or shore.

774 DAVILA – From the village.

776 WHITEHEAD – Descriptional surname for someone with white or very light blonde hair.

777 PRUITT – From the Old French "proux" meaning valiant or brave one.

778 KENT – From Kent, England or literally "from the coast."

779 CONWAY – Irish surname from "Mac Connmhaigh," a descriptional surname meaning "Head Smasher" or "Mac Connbhuidhe," meaning "yellow hound"

780 McKEE – From the Gaelic surname "Mac Aodh," literally meaning "son of the fiery one."

781 BARR – From the great hill.

782 DAVID – Beloved.

783 DEJESUS – Follower of Jesus Christ.

784 MARIN – Family of Marino or "lives near the sea."

785 BERGER – Either Swedish surname for someone who lived near a hill or mountain, or French for a shepherd (Bergere).

786 McINTYRE – Son of the carpenter or craftsman.

787 BLANKENSHIP – From the hill with a cairn.

788 GAINES – Nickname surname for someone who was very clever. From the word engaingne (ingenuity).

789 PALACIOS – Spanish surname for someone who lived in a palace or worked in a palace.

790 CUEVAS – Habitational surname for someone who lived in or near caves.

791 BARTLETT – Son or family of Bartholomew.

792 DURHAM – Habitational surname for a family from Durham, U.K. literally meaning "by the hill."

793 DORSEY – From the village of Arcy in La Manche, France.

794 McCALL – From Gaelic surname "Mac Cathmhaoil," literally meaning "son of the battle chief."

795 O'DONNELL – Family of Donnell/Donald.

796 STEIN – Family of Stephen.

797 BROWNING – Descriptive surname from the Olde English "brun" meaning someone with brown hair or skin.

798 STOUT – Bold one.

799 LOWERY – Family of Lawrence.

800 SLOAN – From the old Gaelic given name "Sluaghadhan," meaning a leader of a military expedition.

801 McLEAN – From the old Gaelic name "Mac gille Eoin," literally meaning "son of the devotee of Saint John."

802 HENDRICKS – Family of Hendrick/Heinrich.

803 CALHOUN – Variant of the Scottish surname, Colquhoun, meaning "nook" or "corner."

804 SEXTON – Occupational surname for someone who worked as a sexton, a warden of a church.

805 CHUNG – Chinese/Korean surname literally meaning "hanging bell flower."

806 GENTRY – Born of high status.

807 HULL – Either a habitational surname for someone who lived on or near a hill, or from the given name Hulle, which was a nickname for Hugh.

808 DUARTE – A prosperous guardian.

809 ELLISON – Son of Ellis/Elias/Elijah.

810 NIELSEN – Son of Niel.

811 GILLESPIE – From the Gaelic "Mac giolla Easpuig," meaning "son of the bishop's servant."

812 BUCK – Either descriptive or occupational surname for someone who resembled a male deer, or someone who traded in them.

813 MIDDLETON – From anyone of the places named Middleton in the UK, literally meaning "the middle town."

814 SELLERS – Occupational surname for someone who was a merchant/seller.

815 LEBLANC – French surname for someone who was pale or had very blond hair.

816 ESPARZA – Occupational surname for a professional swordsman/soldier.

817 HARDIN – Habitational surname for families from any number of towns in England named Harden/Hardin. Literally means "valley of the hare."

818 BRADSHAW – From the broad grove.

819 McINTOSH – Son of the chief, leader.

820 HOWE – Lives near a man-made mound or burial mound.

821 LIVINGSTON – From the town founded by Leving (given name). Scottish clan name.

822 FROST – Nickname surname for a person who had white hair or who had a 'frosty' disposition.

823 GLASS – Occupational surname for a glass blower.

824 MORSE – Family of Maurice. Literally means dark or swarthy person (from Moor).

825 KNAPP – Hilltop.

826 HERMAN – Army man.

827 STARK – Unwielding, steady, firm.

828 BRAVO – Brave, proven in battle.

829 NOBLE – From nobility. High born.

830 SPEARS – Occupational surname for a keeper of the Watch, which was an early form of a police officer.

831 WEEKS – Is from or works in a dairy farm, from the old English word "wic."

832 CORONA – Literally means crown, but could mean several occupations: someone who made helmets or hats, someone who was going bald, or a follower of Christianity referring to the crown of thorns.

833 FREDERICK – Peace ruler.

834 BUCKLEY – Lives near the goat clearing.

835 McFARLAND – Scottish surname from the Gaelic "MacPharlain" meaning "son of Parlan."

836 HEBERT – Illustrious soldier.

837 ENRIQUEZ – Son of Enrique.

838 HICKMAN – Occupational surname for a servant of a man called Hick.

839 QUINTERO – Spanish surname meaning "fifth" or a person from Quintero in Ourense province, from the word quinteiro, meaning "farmstead."

840 RANDOLPH – Shield Wolf.

841 SCHAEFER – German occupational surname from the word "schäfer" which means "shepherd."

842 WALLS – Someone who lived near or behind a big wall.

843 TREJO – Habitational Spanish surname, for someone from Trexo, a place in Asturias in northwest Spain.

844 HOUSE – Habitational or occupational surname for someone who either owned a big mansion or worked in one.

845 REILLY – Gaelic name from O'Reilly, meaning son or descendent of Raghailligh.

846 PENNINGTON – From the town with a livestock enclosure.

847 MICHAEL – Who is like god?

848 CONRAD – Brave counsel.

849 GILES – Holy man or one who does good.

850 BENJAMIN – Son of my right hand.

851 CROSBY – Lives by the cross or crossing.

852 FITZPATRICK – Son of Patrick

853 DONOVAN – From the Irish surname Donnabhain, a diminutive/nickname for someone with darker skin or wore brown.

854 MAYS – Either family of Matthew or a nickname for a guy who is a good friend.

855 MAHONEY – From the Gaelic surname "O'Mathghamhana" meaning "son of Mathghamhain," literally meaning "bear."

856 VALENTINE – Strong, healthy, valiant.

857 RAYMOND – Counsel protection.

858 MEDRANO – Abundance.

859 HAHN – German surname from the word "hane" meaning "rooster," applied as a nickname for a conceited or sexually active man.

860 McMILLAN – From the Gaelic surname "Macghillemhaoil," meaning son of the monk's servant.

861 SMALL – Person who is short or small.

862 BENTLEY – From the clearing overgrown with bent-grass.

863 FELIX – Originally a term of endearment, meant "happy one."

864 PECK – Occupational surname for someone who dealt in "pekkes"–a medieval measure of dry goods equal to 28 pounds.

865 LUCERO – Light or evening star.

866 BOYLE – From the Gaelic surname "O'Baoighill," meaning "family of the rash or angry person."

867 HANNA – From the Gaelic "O'hannaigh," meaning "descendant of Annach" literally meaning "iniquity."

868 PACE – The peaceful one. Could have been used as a cynical nickname for someone who was not.

869 RUSH – From the place with reeds or occupational surname for someone who worked with reeds.

870 HURLEY – From the village on cleared land.

871 HARDING – Son of the hardened one. Hardened meaning battled in war.

872 McCONNELL – From the Gaelic "MacDhomhnuill" meaning son of Donald/Donal.

873 BERNAL – Spanish surname meaning "son of Baruch."

874 NAVA – Habitational surname from many towns named Nava in Spain, literally meaning "treeless plateau."

875 AYERS – Heir to a fortune or land.

876 EVERETT – Herd of wild boars.

877 VENTURA – Foundling or deserted child – used for someone who was innocent or gullible.

878 AVERY – Elf king.

879 PUGH – Welsh surname from "ap Hugh" meaning "son of Hugh."

880 MAYER – Occupational surname for a mayor of a village or town.

881 BENDER – German occupational surname for a barrel maker.

882 SHEPARD – Occupational surname for a shepherd.

883 McMAHON – From the Gaelic surname "Mac Mathghamha," which means "son of the Bear."

884 LANDRY – Land ruler.

885 CASE – Occupational surname for someone who makes boxes, cases, or chests.

886 SAMPSON – The sun.

887 MOSES – Born of a god.

888 MAGANA – Habitational name from either of the villages named Magaña, in Soria and Córdoba provinces in Spain.

889 BLACKBURN – Lives near the dark colored stream.

890 DUNLAP – From the fort by the muddy place.

891 GOULD – Descriptional surname for someone with "golden" hair or occupational for someone who worked with gold, like a jewelry maker or gilder.

892 DUFFY – From the Gaelic surname "Mac Dhubhshith" meaning "son of the peaceful black one."

893 VAUGHAN – Welsh descriptional surname meaning "small, little."

894 HERRING – Occupational surname for a fisher or seller of herring (fish).

895 McKAY – From the Gaelic surname "MacAodh," literally meaning "son of fire."

896 ESPINOSA – Lives by the thorn bushes or a person with a "prickly" character.

897 RIVERS – Lives by the river.

898 FARLEY – Habitational surname for one who is from any of the many English towns called Farley or Farleigh. Literally means "fern-covered clearing."

899 BERNARD – Bold as a bear.

900 ASHLEY – From the ash wood or clearing.

901 FRIEDMAN – Servant of god or friend.

902 POTTS – Family of Philpott, an early form of the name Phillip.

903 TRUONG – Vietnamese surname meaning "drawing a bow" or archer.

904 COSTA – Someone from the coast or a bank of a river.

905 CORREA – Occupational surname for someone who made or sold leather straps.

906 BLEVINS – Welsh surname from the word "Blaid" meaning wolf.

907 NIXON – Son of Nick/Nicholas.

908 CLEMENTS – Family of Clement.

909 FRY – Born free.

910 DELAROSA – From the family of Rose, or from an area where wild roses grew.

911 BEST – Occupational surname for someone who was a cattle-herder or dealer. From the old English "beste" meaning "beast."

912 BENTON – From the town with the bent grass.

913 LUGO – Habitational surname for families from the town of Lugo in Galicia, Spain. Literally means "from the wood grove of Augustus."

914 PORTILLO – Spanish/Castilian surname meaning "small port."

915 DOUGHERTY – From the Gaelic surname "O'Dochartaigh," meaning "descendent of the hurtful one."

916 CRANE – Nickname surname given to a man who was tall and thin like a crane (bird).

917 HALEY – From the hay clearing.

918 PHAN – Vietnamese surname of unknown meaning.

919 VILLALOBOS – From the town of Villalobos, Spain, meaning "the village of wolves."

920 BLANCHARD – With white hair or pale complexion.

921 HORNE – Occupational surname for someone who carved objects out of horn, or made musical horns (usually made out of animal horn at the time).

922 FINLEY – From the Gaelic surname "Fionlagh," meaning "fair hero."

923 QUINTANA – Country house.

924 LYNN – Most likely a habitational surname from the Welsh word "llyn" meaning "lake."

925 ESQUIVEL – Behind the lime tree.

926 BEAN – Either from the word "bene" meaning "friend, good person" or occupational for someone who literally grew or sold beans.

927 DODSON – Son of Dodd.

928 MULLEN – Lives at or near a mill.

929 XIONG – Chinese surname meaning "bear."

930 HAYDEN – From the hedge enclosure, down hill.

931 CANO – Spanish/Portugal surname referring to a cave, or a French/Italian occupational surname occupational for someone who supplied cane/reeds for thatching.

932 LEVY – From the family of Levi.

933 HUBER – German surname for the word "hide," a unit of farm land.

934 RICHMOND – Habitational surname from any of the towns in England or northern France with that name. Literally means "From the rich hill or mount."

935 MOYER – From the ancient Gaelic surname "Mac an Mhaoir" meaning "steward, assistant, right-hand man."

936 LIM – Chinese surname meaning "forest."

937 FRYE – Born free.

938 SHEPPARD – Occupational surname for a shepherd.

939 McCARTY – From the Gaelic surname "Mac Carthaigh" meaning "son of the loving one."

940 AVALOS – Spanish habitational surname for someone from Ábalos, Spain. Unknown meaning.

941 BOOKER – Occupational surname for someone who bound, wrote, or sold books.

942 WALLER – Either a habitational surname for someone who lived near a stone wall, or occupational for someone who built walls/was a mason.

943 PARRA – Spanish/Portuguese surname, meaning "grapevine/trellis." Possibly used for someone who grew grapes or had a winery.

944 WOODWARD – Ward of the forest/woods.

945 JARAMILLO – Spanish Habitatonal surname for someone from the south of Castilla, Spain, literally referring to a "jaramago tree."

946 KRUEGER – German occupational surname for someone who made or sold glass/pottery "kruog," or ran an inn "krug."

947 RASMUSSEN – Danish/Norwegian surname, meaning "son of Rasmus."

948 BRANDT – Family of Brando, literally meaning "hot-tempered."

949 PERALTA – Habitational surname for someone from any number of places named Peralta in Spain. Literally means "high rock."

950 DONALDSON – Son of Donald.

951 STUART – Occupational surname for someone who worked as a steward/assistant.

952 FAULKNER – Occupational surname for a falconer or someone who trained hawks/falcons.

953 MAYNARD – Strength, strong.

954 GALINDO – Spanish surname of unknown meaning.

955 COFFEY – From the Gaelic surname "O Cobhthaigh" meaning "descendant of the victorious."

956 ESTES – From the East.

957 SANFORD – From the sandy ford.

958 BURCH – Lives near the birch tree or grove.

959 MADDOX – From the ancient Welsh male name "Matoc" meaning "good fortune."

960 VO – Vietnamese surname meaning "fighter/soldier."

961 O'CONNELL – Descendant of Conaill.

962 VU – Vietnamese surname meaning "fighter/soldier."

963 ANDERSEN – Son of Anders/Andrew.

964 SPENCE – Occupational surname for someone in charge of a pantry/goods in an estate.

965 McPHERSON – From the Gaelic surname "Mac an Phearsain," meaning "son of the parson."

966 CHURCH – Someone who worked in a church or lived near a church.

967 SCHMITT – German occupational surname for a smith/metalworker.

968 STANTON – From the village on stony ground.

969 LEAL – Loyal one.

970 CHERRY – Occupational surname for someone who grew or sold cherries.

971 COMPTON – From the valley farm.

972 DUDLEY – From "Dudda's clearing" – Dudda was a nickname for a rotund/heavy person.

973 SIERRA – Spanish surname meaning "mountain range" used for families living in or near the Galicia and Asturias regions of northern Spain.

974 POLLARD – Strong descendent of Paul.

975 ALFARO – Spanish habitational surname for someone from Alfaro, Spain in the Logroño province. Literally means "the beacon/lighthouse."

976 HESTER – Either lives by the beech tree, or an occupational surname for a herald/town crier.

977 PROCTOR – Occupational surname for a proctor/manager/attorney.

978 LU – Chinese surname of unknown meaning.

979 HINTON – From the high enclosure/settlement.

980 NOVAK – The newcomer/new one.

981 GOOD – Respected/good person.

982 MADDEN – From the Irish surname "O'Madain," meaning "descendant of the son of the hound."

983 McCANN – From the Gaelic surname "MacCana," meaning "descendant of the wolf cub."

983 TERRELL – Stubborn one.

985 JARVIS – From the given name Gervase meaning "spear" or "spear/valley."

986 DICKSON – Son of Richard.

987 REYNA – From the French surname "Rainer" meaning "army counsel."

988 CANTRELL – Occupational surname for a bell ringer (someone who rang the Chanterelles) or who sang in a choir.

989 MAYO – From the family of Matthew.

990 BRANCH – Possibly a habitational surname for someone from Branch, a land division in Wiltshire, U.K. or from Branches Park, a former country mansion in West Suffolk, U.K.

991 HENDRIX – Family of Heinrich.

992 ROLLINS – Family of Rollo.

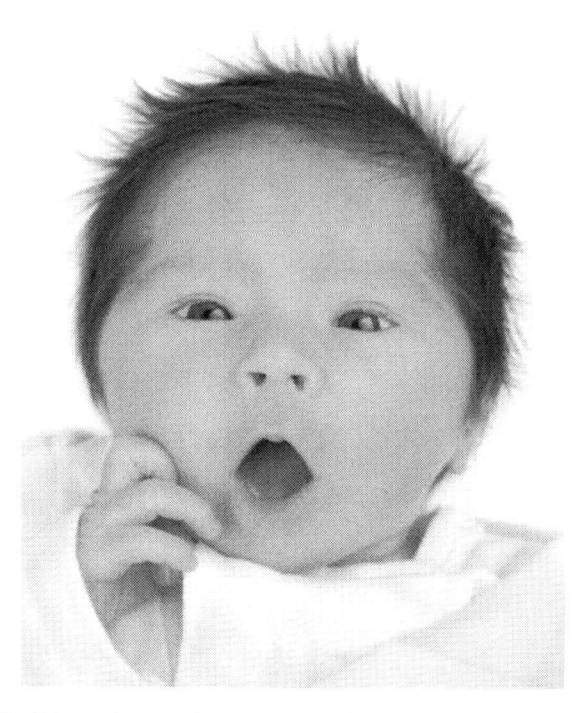

993 ROWLAND – From the renowned land.

994 WHITNEY – From the land surrounded by streams.

995 DUKE – Leader (of an army or troops).

996 ODOM – Son-in-law of a prominent person.

997 DAUGHERTY – From the Gaelic surname "O'Dochartaigh," meaning "descendent of the hurtful one."

998 TRAVIS – Occupational surname for someone who collected a tax or toll at a crossing.

999 TANG – Vietnamese surname, meaning "from the Tang dynasty."

1000 ARCHER – Occupational surname for an archer/bow man.

Top 300 Baby Girl Names in the U.S

Choosing a great name for your daughter is a big responsibility. While it's certainly a fun experience, it can be stressful, too! After all, naming your baby girl is one of the first and most important decisions you will make as a new parent.

If you're like most parents on their search for a perfect girl name, you may be hoping to incorporate special meaning, honor a family or cultural tradition, or find a name that's unique on its own.

Whatever your approach, this list of the 300 most popular baby girl names, as recorded by the Social Security Administration (SSA), will help you consider all your options, enjoy the experience, and narrow down your list to a favorite choice. The following list reflects the U.S. birth certificate data from 2019.

Top 300 Baby Girl Names of 2019

1. Olivia
2. Emma
3. Ava
4. Sophia
5. Isabella
6. Charlotte
7. Amelia
8. Mia
9. Harper
10. Evelyn
11. Abigail
12. Emily
13. Ella
14. Elizabeth
15. Camila
16. Luna
17. Sofia
18. Avery
19. Mila
20. Aria
21. Scarlett
22. Penelope
23. Layla
24. Chloe
25. Victoria
26. Madison
27. Eleanor
28. Grace
29. Nora
30. Riley
31. Zoey
32. Hannah
33. Hazel
34. Lily
35. Ellie
36. Violet
37. Lillian
38. Zoe
39. Stella
40. Aurora
41. Natalie
42. Emilia
43. Everly
44. Leah
45. Aubrey
46. Willow
47. Addison
48. Lucy
49. Audrey
50. Bella
51. Nova
52. Brooklyn
53. Paisley
54. Savannah
55. Claire
56. Skylar
57. Isla
58. Genesis
59. Naomi
60. Elena
61. Caroline
62. Eliana
63. Anna
64. Maya
65. Valentina
66. Ruby
67. Kennedy
68. Ivy
69. Ariana
70. Aaliyah
71. Cora
72. Madelyn
73. Alice
74. Kinsley
75. Hailey
76. Gabriella
77. Allison
78. Gianna
79. Serenity
80. Samantha
81. Sarah
82. Autumn
83. Quinn
84. Eva
85. Piper
86. Sophie
87. Sadie
88. Delilah
89. Josephine
90. Nevaeh

91. Adeline	121. Katherine	151. Eloise
92. Arya	122. Aubree	152. Emerson
93. Emery	123. Adalynn	153. Cecilia
94. Lydia	124. Kylie	154. Remi
95. Clara	125. Faith	155. Josie
96. Vivian	126. Mary	156. Alina
97. Madeline	127. Margaret	157. Reese
98. Peyton	128. Ximena	158. Bailey
99. Julia	129. Iris	159. Lucia
100. Rylee	130. Alexandra	160. Adalyn
101. Brielle	131. Jasmine	161. Molly
102. Reagan	132. Charlie	162. Ayla
103. Natalia	133. Amaya	163. Sara
104. Jade	134. Taylor	164. Daisy
105. Athena	135. Isabel	165. London
106. Maria	136. Ashley	166. Jordyn
107. Leilani	137. Khloe	167. Esther
108. Everleigh	138. Ryleigh	168. Genevieve
109. Liliana	139. Alexa	169. Harmony
110. Melanie	140. Amara	170. Annabelle
111. Mackenzie	141. Valeria	171. Alyssa
112. Hadley	142. Andrea	172. Ariel
113. Raelynn	143. Parker	173. Aliyah
114. Kaylee	144. Norah	174. Londyn
115. Rose	145. Eden	175. Juliana
116. Arianna	146. Elliana	176. Morgan
117. Isabelle	147. Brianna	177. Summer
118. Melody	148. Emersyn	178. Juliette
119. Eliza	149. Valerie	179. Trinity
120. Lyla	150. Anastasia	180. Callie

181. Sienna
182. Blakely
183. Alaia
184. Kayla
185. Teagan
186. Alaina
187. Brynlee
188. Finley
189. Catalina
190. Sloane
191. Rachel
192. Lilly
193. Ember
194. Kimberly
195. Juniper
196. Sydney
197. Arabella
198. Gemma
199. Jocelyn
200. Freya
201. June
202. Lauren
203. Amy
204. Presley
205. Georgia
206. Journee
207. Elise
208. Rosalie
209. Ada
210. Laila

211. Brooke
212. Diana
213. Olive
214. River
215. Payton
216. Ariella
217. Daniela
218. Raegan
219. Alayna
220. Gracie
221. Mya
222. Blake
223. Noelle
224. Ana
225. Leila
226. Paige
227. Lila
228. Nicole
229. Rowan
230. Hope
231. Ruth
232. Alana
233. Selena
234. Marley
235. Kamila
236. Alexis
237. Mckenzie
238. Zara
239. Millie
240. Magnolia

241. Kali
242. Kehlani
243. Catherine
244. Maeve
245. Adelyn
246. Sawyer
247. Elsie
248. Lola
249. Jayla
250. Adriana
251. Journey
252. Vera
253. Aspen
254. Joanna
255. Alivia
256. Angela
257. Dakota
258. Camille
259. Nyla
260. Tessa
261. Brooklynn
262. Malia
263. Makayla
264. Rebecca
265. Fiona
266. Mariana
267. Lena
268. Julianna
269. Vanessa
270. Juliet

271. Camilla
272. Kendall
273. Harley
274. Cali
275. Evangeline
276. Mariah
277. Jane
278. Zuri
279. Elaina
280. Sage
281. Amira
282. Adaline
283. Lia
284. Charlee
285. Delaney
286. Lilah
287. Miriam
288. Angelina
289. Mckenna
290. Aniyah
291. Phoebe
292. Michelle
293. Thea
294. Hayden
295. Maggie
296. Lucille
297. Amiyah
298. Annie
299. Alexandria
300. Myla

Top 300 Baby Boy Names in the U.S

Top Baby Names for Boys

Elijah, Jacob, Noah, Benjamin, James, Mason, William, Logan, Oliver, Liam

Finding the perfect name for your new baby boy can take some time and careful consideration, but it can also be a lot of fun. In fact, it's one of the first and biggest decisions you have to make as a new parent.

Are you looking for a boy name that speaks to a family tradition or honors a cultural tradition? Or do you want your son to have a completely unique name?

Whatever your approach, you'll find plenty of great options in the following list of the 300 most popular baby boy names, as recorded by the Social Security Administration (SSA). The following list reflects the U.S. birth certificate data from 2019.

Baby Names and Meanings

Take a look through to help you narrow down your list of favorites (or inspire new ones) and enjoy the experience of finding a name you love for your new son.

Top 300 Baby Boy Names of 2019

1. Liam
2. Noah
3. Oliver
4. William
5. Elijah
6. James
7. Benjamin
8. Lucas
9. Mason
10. Ethan
11. Alexander
12. Henry
13. Jacob
14. Michael
15. Daniel
16. Logan
17. Jackson
18. Sebastian
19. Jack
20. Aiden
21. Owen
22. Samuel
23. Matthew
24. Joseph
25. Levi
26. Mateo
27. David
28. John
29. Wyatt
30. Carter
31. Julian
32. Luke
33. Grayson
34. Isaac
35. Jayden
36. Theodore
37. Gabriel
38. Anthony
39. Dylan
40. Leo
41. Lincoln
42. Jaxon
43. Asher
44. Christopher
45. Josiah
46. Andrew
47. Thomas
48. Joshua
49. Ezra
50. Hudson
51. Charles
52. Caleb
53. Isaiah
54. Ryan
55. Nathan
56. Adrian
57. Christian
58. Maverick
59. Colton
60. Elias
61. Aaron
62. Eli
63. Landon
64. Jonathan
65. Nolan
66. Hunter
67. Cameron
68. Connor
69. Santiago
70. Jeremiah
71. Ezekiel
72. Angel
73. Roman
74. Easton
75. Miles
76. Robert
77. Jameson
78. Nicholas

79. Greyson	109. Brooks	139. Ivan
80. Cooper	110. Micah	140. Brandon
81. Ian	111. Damian	141. Jonah
82. Carson	112. Harrison	142. Giovanni
83. Axel	113. Waylon	143. Kaiden
84. Jaxson	114. Ayden	144. Myles
85. Dominic	115. Vincent	145. Calvin
86. Leonardo	116. Ryder	146. Lorenzo
87. Luca	117. Kingston	147. Maxwell
88. Austin	118. Rowan	148. Jayce
89. Jordan	119. George	149. Kevin
90. Adam	120. Luis	150. Legend
91. Xavier	121. Chase	151. Tristan
92. Jose	122. Cole	152. Jesus
93. Jace	123. Nathaniel	153. Jude
94. Everett	124. Zachary	154. Zion
95. Declan	125. Ashton	155. Justin
96. Evan	126. Braxton	156. Maddox
97. Kayden	127. Gavin	157. Abel
98. Parker	128. Tyler	158. King
99. Wesley	129. Diego	159. Camden
100. Kai	130. Bentley	160. Elliott
101. Brayden	131. Amir	161. Malachi
102. Bryson	132. Beau	162. Milo
103. Weston	133. Gael	163. Emmanuel
104. Jason	134. Carlos	164. Karter
105. Emmett	135. Ryker	165. Rhett
106. Sawyer	136. Jasper	166. Alex
107. Silas	137. Max	167. August
108. Bennett	138. Juan	168. River

169. Xander
170. Antonio
171. Brody
172. Finn
173. Elliot
174. Dean
175. Emiliano
176. Eric
177. Miguel
178. Arthur
179. Matteo
180. Graham
181. Alan
182. Nicolas
183. Blake
184. Thiago
185. Adriel
186. Victor
187. Joel
188. Timothy
189. Hayden
190. Judah
191. Abraham
192. Edward
193. Messiah
194. Zayden
195. Theo
196. Tucker
197. Grant
198. Richard

199. Alejandro
200. Steven
201. Jesse
202. Dawson
203. Bryce
204. Avery
205. Oscar
206. Patrick
207. Archer
208. Barrett
209. Leon
210. Colt
211. Charlie
212. Peter
213. Kaleb
214. Lukas
215. Beckett
216. Jeremy
217. Preston
218. Enzo
219. Luka
220. Andres
221. Marcus
222. Felix
223. Mark
224. Ace
225. Brantley
226. Atlas
227. Remington
228. Maximus

229. Matias
230. Walker
231. Kyrie
232. Griffin
233. Kenneth
234. Israel
235. Javier
236. Kyler
237. Jax
238. Amari
239. Zane
240. Emilio
241. Knox
242. Adonis
243. Aidan
244. Kaden
245. Paul
246. Omar
247. Brian
248. Louis
249. Caden
250. Maximiliano
251. Holden
252. Paxton
253. Nash
254. Bradley
255. Bryan
256. Simon
257. Phoenix
258. Lane

259. Josue
260. Colin
261. Rafael
262. Kyle
263. Riley
264. Jorge
265. Beckham
266. Cayden
267. Jaden
268. Emerson
269. Ronan
270. Karson
271. Arlo
272. Tobias
273. Brady
274. Clayton
275. Francisco
276. Zander
277. Erick
278. Walter
279. Daxton
280. Cash
281. Martin
282. Damien
283. Dallas
284. Cody
285. Chance
286. Jensen
287. Finley
288. Jett
289. Corbin
290. Kash
291. Reid
292. Kameron
293. Andre
294. Gunner
295. Jake
296. Hayes
297. Manuel
298. Prince
299. Bodhi
300. Cohen

5 Naming Trends From Around The World

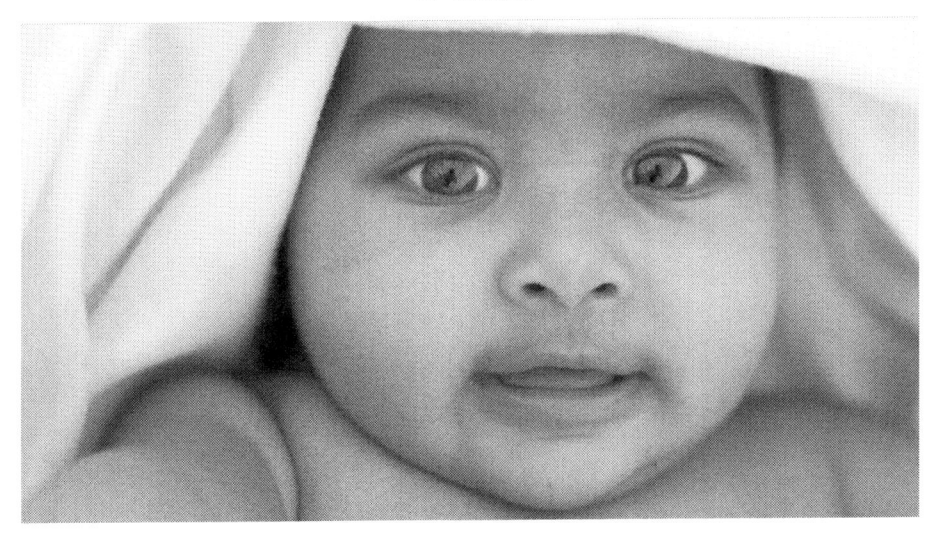

Every parent across the globe has a different way of coming up with the perfect name for their baby.

Cultural influences certainly play their part, but there are some baby-naming trends that are strong enough to cross national borders. Read on to discover our top five global baby-naming trends.

1. Celebrity names

In the UK, US, and Brazil, fame counts!

For example, Benjamin raced up the Brazilian baby name charts after supermodel Gisele Bundchen chose it for her first baby. In the US, Matthew McConaughey's choice of Levi for his son saw the name jump in popularity. While in the UK, Anthony has shot into the top

100 after Wayne and Coleen Rooney chose it as their younger son's middle name.

2. Traditional names

In some countries, traditional, old-fashioned names are favourites. In Russia, the same names have been popular for centuries. Traditional names, such as Dmitry, Anastasia, Ivan and Anna, all keep their top 10 status, year after year.

Traditional names also dominate in Germany, Switzerland, and Austria. Short, biblical names such as Ben, Jonas, and Noah remain popular for boys. Names with a Greek root, such as Leon and Lukas, are also popular. For girls, traditional names that won't date, such as Emma, Marie, Johanna, Emilia, and Anna, keep going strong.

3. Religious names

In Spain and the Philippines, the Roman Catholic faith binds together family and society. Parents often choose Spanish spellings of biblical names or saints' names for their children. These can be either as first names or as middle names, or both.

For example, the popular boys' name Manuel is derived from the Hebrew name Emmanuel, meaning "God is with us". And favoured girls' name Marta is from the Aramaic name Martha.

In Arab countries, parents following the Islamic faith favour virtuous names that honour the prophets. By picking these names, parents hope to inspire a righteous life and bring blessings to their baby. The names of prophets such as Mohammed, Ali, and Ibrahim are all popular. Mohammed is also the number-one boys' name in Malaysia, where Islam is the most-practised religion.

4. Names with special meanings

In some countries, the meaning of the name is the most important consideration. In India, parents often consult horoscopes to gain an insight into the kind of personality their baby will develop as she grows. This helps them to choose a name with a meaning that corresponds to their baby's birth star. It is believed that choosing your baby's name based on her birth star plays a significant role in shaping her character and destiny.

In China, the two or three characters that make up a baby's name must combine in a way that brings good luck and prosperity to the child. Parents like to choose a baby's name that reflects either masculine or feminine qualities. So boys' names are linked with strength and firmness, and girls' names with beauty and flowers.

5. Names based on nature

India is clearly a nation that celebrates nature. Names inspired by the sun, such as Vivaan and Vihaan, have a strong presence in the baby name charts. Also popular is Arnav, meaning ocean, and Darsh, meaning moonlight.

In Australia, Canada, the UK, and the US, names inspired by parents' growing eco-awareness are becoming more popular. Flower or plant names such as Daisy, Lily, Ivy, and Poppy are in style for girls. For boys, Storm, Forrest, and River have been making an impact.

Printed in Great Britain
by Amazon